Your *Secret FREE Bonus!*

As a preferred client of Afflatus Publishing we strive to provide more value, all the time. As you are now a special part of our family we want to let you in on a little a little secret...

A special thanks goes out to you. So subscribe to our free e-book giveaway. Each week we will spotlight an amazing new title. *Yours absolutely free.*

Subscribe For Free Now http://bit.ly/1aj9JHs

W0006991

Table of Contents

Top 80 Chinese Appetizer, Main Dish, One Dish, Dessert, Salad, Soup, Lunch And Snack Recipes

Chinese Appetizer Meals

Chinese Main Dish Meals

Chinese Salad Meals

Chinese Lunch and Snack Meals

Chinese One Dish Meals

Chinese Dessert Meals

Chinese Soup Meals

Chinese Appetizer Meals

Chinese Latkes with Tangy Dipping Sauce

Ingredients

- For Latkes
- 2 medium potatoes
- 3 green onions, finely chopped
- 1 egg
- 1 1/2 tablespoons cornstarch
- 1 teaspoon salt
- 2 tablespoons vegetable oil
- For Chinese Dipping Sauce
- 1 teaspoon sesame seeds

- 1 clove garlic, minced
- 1 green onion, finely chopped
- 4 tablespoons soy sauce
- 2 tablespoons white vinegar
- 2 teaspoons sesame oil
- 1 teaspoon sugar

Directions

1. First of all, take potatoes, grate them and mix these grated potatoes with green onions.
2. Beat the eggs. Blend in cornstarch. Blend in salt
3. Take egg mixture and pour this into potatoes, coat well.
4. Drop the potato mixture by tablespoonful's in one tablespoon of oil in sauté pan over moderately high temperature setting and flatten them
5. Cook for FOUR min per side or till become golden in color. Drain properly well.
6. For preparing sauce, toast the sesame seeds over moderately high temperature till slightly brown in color, mixing the pan frequently.
7. Take seeds and mix with the other items.
8. You can serve this delicious recipe with latkes.

Peking Duck

Ingredients

- 1 (5 lb) duck
- 2 teaspoons salt
- 1/3 cup vodka
- 3 tablespoons honey
- 3 cups water
- 6 slices fresh ginger
- For serving:
- to taste Mandarin pancake
- to taste green onion, ends sliced to make a brush
- to taste hoisin sauce
- 1 cucumber, peeled and cut in slivers

Directions

1. First of all, take duck and wash it and then dry it both the inside and outside.

2. After this, rub the salt into cavity.

3. Place the duck on a dish.

4. Spoon the vodka all over duck.

5. And rub the whole duck.

6. Then let it rest for FOUR hrs.

7. Take honey and dissolve in water and after this, rub this all over duck.

8. Let it dry for a minimum of FOUR hrs.

9. Put ginger inside duck.

10. Then put duck on rack in pan along with water in it. Keep the duck above water.

11. Cook for ½ hour at 375 and lower the temperature to 3oo and keep on roasting for 60 min

12. Then raise the temperature to 375 and keep on roasting till skin become crunchy and brown in color all over.

Three Delicious Chinese Sauces

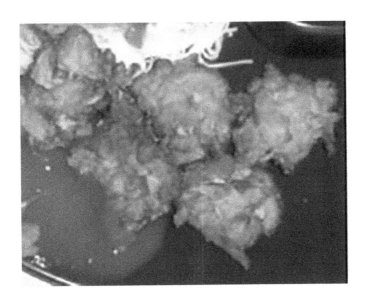

Ingredients

GINGER-SCALLION SAUCE RECIPE

- 2 tablespoons grated ginger
- 2 spring scallions, very finely chopped
- 1/4-1/2 teaspoon salt
- 1 -2 tablespoon peanut oil
- 1 tablespoon sesame oil

GARLIC AND GREEN PEPPER OR HOT CHILI PEPPER SAUCE RECIPE

- 2 -3 tablespoons of finely chopped green peppers
- 2 cloves garlic, crushed
- 1/4 teaspoon sugar

- 2 tablespoons peanut oil
- 2 tablespoons soy sauce
- 1 tablespoon red rice vinegar
- 1 tablespoon sesame oil

OYSTER SAUCE RECIPE

- 1 tablespoon light soy sauce
- 2 tablespoons oyster sauce
- 1 tablespoon peanut oil
- 1 tablespoon soup stock

Directions

1. For the preparation of ginger scallion sauce; take the ginger and mix with salt and scallions and put in a dish.
2. Heat two oils. After this, pour this over G-S mixture and mix.
3. Add the rest of items according to your own choice and taste.
4. Before adding the heated oil, add one tsp of soy sauce, one tsp of fish sauce, pinch of white pepper.
5. For preparation of garlic and green pepper sauce; take green pepper and mix with sugar, and garlic in a dish.
6. Heat the peanut oil and pour this over the mixture.
7. Add the remaining items and blend well. And put aside for ½ hour.
8. For the preparation of oyster sauce; blend all of the items.

Chinese Chicken in Foil Appetizers

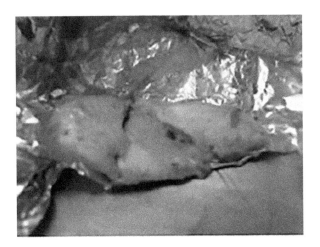

Ingredients

- PAPER WRAPPED CHICKEN
- 1 1/2 lbs. boneless skinless chicken breasts
- 2 green onions, finely chopped
- 40 -50 pieces aluminum foil, cut into 5 x 6 inches
- 1 tablespoon hoisin sauce
- 1 tablespoon soy sauce
- 1 tablespoon sherry wine
- 1 tablespoon oil
- 1 teaspoon sesame oil
- 1 garlic clove, minced
- 1/4 teaspoon pepper
- 1 teaspoon sugar
- 2 teaspoons cornstarch

Directions

1. Chop the chicken into pieces
2. Then put in shallow pan and use green onions as sprinkle over the top.
3. Blend all of the marinade items and pour all over chicken.
4. Allow to marinate for 120 minutes.
5. Wrap each chicken piece in square and put in one layer on cookie sheet.
6. Bake for TWELVE minutes at 450 degrees Fahrenheit.

Chinese Fragrant Spareribs

Ingredients

- 1/3 cup soy sauce
- 1/3 cup plum jelly
- 3 tablespoons water
- 2 tablespoons dry sherry
- 2 garlic cloves, minced
- 1 teaspoon five-spice powder
- 2 lbs. pork baby back ribs, cut into single ribs

Directions

1. Take the soy sauce, plum jelly and whisk them together with water, sherry, garlic and 5 spice powder till jelly is mixed and dissolved.

2. Let the mixture to cool.

3. Pour this mixture into Ziploc bag and then add in ribs.

4. After this, seal the bag. And coat the ribs with the sauce.

5. Let them marinate for a minimum of THREE hrs.

6. Then put these ribs on baking pan that has been lined with foil.

7. Use the foil for covering, preserve the marinade.

8. Bake for ½ hour at FOUR FIFTY (45o) degrees Fahrenheit.

9. Take the ribs out of oven and remove the top foil.

10. Right after this, drain the liquids from baking pan and turn these ribs.

11. After this, bake the ribs for approximately ¼ to ½ hour at THREE FIFTY (35o) degrees Fahrenheit or till ribs are cooked through.

12. Use the preserved marinade for basting a couple of times.

Chocolate-Dipped Fortune Cookies

Ingredients

- 1 dozen fortune cookies
- 1/2 cup semi-sweet chocolate chips
- 1 tablespoon shortening

Directions

1. First of all, melt the chocolate chips in bowl.
2. Blend in shortening.
3. After this, dip the cookies in chocolate and put on waxed paper.

Asian Pork Balls with Napa Cabbage

Ingredients

- 2 lbs. ground lean pork
- 2 tablespoons soy sauce
- 1 (8 ounce) cans water chestnuts, minced
- 1/2 cup onion, finely chopped
- 1 teaspoon sesame oil
- 2 teaspoons freshly grated ginger
- Salt and pepper, to taste
- 1 cup chicken broth
- 1 tablespoon soy sauce

- 1 tablespoon sherry wine (optional)
- 6 cups Napa cabbage, thinly sliced
- 1 tablespoon cornstarch
- 2 tablespoons cold water

Directions

1. Blend the 1ˢᵗ 7 items and make balls from the mixture.
2. Put these pork balls on baking sheet.
3. Bake for approximately ½ hour at THREE FIFTY (350) degrees Fahrenheit.
4. Put these balls in large size pot with one cup chicken broth, tbsp. of soy sauce, tbsp. of sherry.
5. Heat to boiling.
6. Lower the temperature, cover and allow to simmer for 1/3 hour.
7. Add in Napa cabbage.
8. Allow to simmer for next, covered, TEN min.
9. Take tbsp. of cornstarch and dissolve into two tbsp. of cold water.
10. Take the pork balls and cabbage out of liquid.
11. Then organize them on a dish.
12. Take cornstarch and blend this into rest of liquid and heat back to boiling.
13. When the sauce become thick, pour this over the pork balls as well as cabbage.

Delicious China Crab Rangoon

Ingredients

- 12 ounces cream cheese, room temperature
- 1/2 teaspoon soy sauce
- 1/4 teaspoon garlic powder
- 2 green onions, minced
- 3/4-1 cup crabmeat, picked
- 50 wonton wrappers
- Oil (for frying)

Directions

1. First of all, mix the green onions, cheese, garlic powder and soy sauce.

2. Blend in crab meat.

3. Put tsp of filling below the center of every wonton wrapper.

4. Roll it up.

5. Use the water for moisten the edges and bring them together over filling and seal.

6. Sauté in heated oil till golden brown in color.

7. Then drain them on kitchen towel.

Sweet and Sour Chicken Wings

Ingredients

- 3 lbs. chicken wings, parts
- 3 beaten eggs
- Cornstarch
- Vegetable oil
- Sauce ingredients
- 1 cup chicken broth
- 2 chicken bouillon cubes
- 1/2 cup catsup
- 1 1/2 cups sugar
- 3/4 cup vinegar
- 2 tablespoons soy sauce
- 1 pinch salt

Directions

1. First of all, dip the chicken parts in eggs. Then after this, dip them in cornstarch.

2. Cook them in oil in sauté pan on both of the sides.

3. Then put them in one layer in baking dish.

4. Heat the sauce items in pan.

5. Take sauce and pour this over the pieces of chicken in the dish.

6. Bake for approximately 60 min at 350 degrees Fahrenheit.

7. Flip over the wings half way through the cooking time period.

Peking Pork Pasta Salad

Ingredients

- 3/4 lb. lean pork, cut into 1/4-inch cubes
- 1 teaspoon vegetable oil
- 6 ounces small-shaped pasta, such as corkscrew, cooked and drained
- 1 lb. fresh spinach leaves, washed and drained
- **Dressing**
- 4 tablespoons soy sauce
- 4 tablespoons sherry wine
- 1 tablespoon sesame oil
- **Garnishes**
- Chopped scallion
- Sliced almonds

Directions

1. Blend the salad items and put aside.
2. Sauté and mix the pork in oil in sauté pan over high temperature setting till brown in color.
3. Take the pork strips and toss with dressing.
4. Take pasta and toss with spinach.
5. Use the pork strips for topping.
6. Use the chopped green onion as garnish along with slices of almond.

Chinese Main Dish Meals

Cantonese Chow Mein

Ingredients

Flavoring mix

- 1 teaspoon salt
- 1 1/2 tablespoons chicken bouillon
- 1 1/2 teaspoons sugar
- 1 1/2 tablespoons oyster sauce
- 1/2 teaspoon sesame oil

Meat ingredients

- 1/2 lb. chicken breast, sliced
- 1/2 lb. barbecued pork
- 6 -8 medium shrimp

Vegetables

- 7 -8 baby bok choy
- Broccoli
- Cauliflower
- 3/4 cup shiitake mushroom
- 1/2 cup sliced bamboo shoot
- 1/4 cup sliced water chestnuts
- 1/2 cup baby corn
- 3 tablespoons minced garlic
- 2 (250 g) packages fresh egg noodles

All other ingredients

- 1/4 cup water
- 1 1/2 tablespoons cornstarch
- 5 tablespoons oil

Directions

1. Take egg noodles and immerse them in boiling water for ½ min. then take out and put aside.
2. Add five tablespoons of oil in sauté pan.
3. Sauté noodles for 120 seconds.
4. Shake the sauté pan back and forth, till noodles become golden brown in color.
5. Turnover and repeat the same process.
6. Take out noodles once noodles become golden in color and become tender on the inner ones and organize these noodles in the middle of a dish.

7. After this, blanch the veggies in boiling water. Then organize the bok choy in circular fashion all around the noodles.

8. Sauté the minced garlic in sauté pan and add blanched veggies and sauté and mix.

9. Add the meat items, one tablespoon of water.

10. Cover the sauté pan and steam for 120 seconds.

11. After this, add in the flavoring items.

12. Add in water with cornstarch.

13. Sauté gently.

14. Take the vegetables and meat AND pour them over noodles.

Sweet and Sour Pork Balls

Ingredients

For The Meat

- 1 lb. ground pork
- 1 tablespoon sesame oil
- 1/3 cup cornstarch
- 1 egg
- 3 tablespoons soy sauce

For The Sauce

- 1 teaspoon cornstarch
- 1/3 cup dry sherry
- 1/3 cup soy sauce

- 1/4 cup tomato paste
- 1/3 cup sugar
- 3 tablespoons white wine vinegar

For The Stir-fry

- 3 tablespoons oil
- 1 cup canned pineapple chunks in syrup
- 1 large onion, coarsely chopped
- 1 green bell pepper, coarsely chopped
- 2 carrots, cut into julienne strips
- Hot steamed rice

Directions

1. Take pork and combine with sesame oil.
2. After this, add cornstarch. Add the egg. And then add the soy sauce. Blend well.
3. After this, prepare meatballs and put them on a dish.
4. After this, prepare the sauce by blending the cold water with cornstarch. After this, add dry sherry.
5. Add in soy sauce.
6. Add in tomato paste. Add in sugar. Add in vinegar. Add in liquid from pineapple. Blend well.
7. **Sauté the meatballs in oil in sauté pan till brown in color. Take out and drain them.**
8. Take carrots, green pepper, and onion and add them to oil in sauté pan and sauté and mix till soft and crunchy.

9. After this, blend the sauce prior to adding to sauté pan and heat all of to boiling, mixing constantly.

10. Take pineapple, meatballs and add them and sauté and mix for a couple of extra min or till all of the items are heated through.

11. You can serve this delicious and exotic recipe with cooked rice.

Honey Spiced Duck

Ingredients

- 2 duck breasts
- 20 ml honey
- 20 ml sherry wine vinegar
- 20 ml soy sauce
- 1 teaspoon freshly grated ginger
- 1 clove garlic, crushed
- 1/4 teaspoon cinnamon
- 1/4 teaspoon Chinese five spice powder
- Freshly ground black pepper
- 8 spring onions

Directions

1. First of all, take the duck breast and score its skin in criss-cross pattern.

2. Take the soy sauce, ginger, garlic, and mix with honey, vinegar and cinnamon, 5 spice powder and pepper in bowl.

3. Then dip duck in the marinade in bowl.

4. Keep in refrigerator, covered, for 60 min.

5. Place in oven at FOUR HUNDRED (400) degrees Fahrenheit in roasting tin, preserve marinade.

6. Cook for approximately ½ hour till cooked.

7. Place the 40 milliliters of roasting juices and marinade in pan.

8. After this, add in spring onions.

9. Heat to boiling.

10. Allow to simmer for 120 seconds.

Hot and Sour Soup

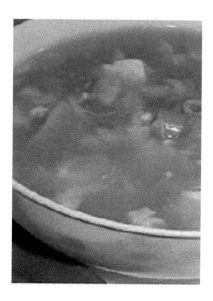

Ingredients

- 4 ounces fresh shiitake mushrooms, stems removed and caps thinly sliced
- 2 fresh garlic cloves, minced
- 2 teaspoons peanut oil or 2 teaspoons cooking oil
- 2 (14 ounce) cans chicken broth
- 2 tablespoons seasoned rice vinegar
- 2 tablespoons reduced sodium soy sauce
- 1 teaspoon chili oil or 1/2 teaspoon crushed red pepper flakes
- 5 ounces cooked chicken breasts, shredded
- 2 cups coleslaw mix, with carrots shredded or 2 cups Napa cabbage, shredded

- 2 tablespoons cold water
- 1 tablespoon cornstarch
- 1 teaspoon toasted sesame oil

Directions

1. First of all, take chicken, cook and shred it and put aside.
2. Cook the garlic and mushrooms in saucepan in oil over moderate temperature for FOUR min, mixing often.
3. Blend in broth. Blend in vinegar. Blend in soy sauce.
4. Blend in red pepper flakes.
5. Heat to boiling.
6. Blend in chicken. Blend in coleslaw mix. Lower the temperature and allow to simmer for FIVE min.
7. Take the cornstarch and mix with water and blend into soup.
8. Allow to simmer for 120 seconds or till become thick slightly.
9. Take away from heat.
10. Blend in sesame oil.

Pineapple Beef Stir-Fry

Ingredients

- 1 (20 ounce) cans pineapple chunks in juice
- 1 tablespoon fresh ginger, grated
- 1 tablespoon soy sauce
- 1/4 cup fresh cilantro, chopped
- 3/4 lb. round steak, thinly sliced diagonal
- 1 teaspoon vegetable oil
- 1 garlic clove, finely chopped
- 1/2 teaspoon cornstarch
- 1/2 cup fresh trimmed green beans
- 1 sweet red pepper, sliced thin
- 2 scallions, chopped
- 1 tablespoon canned chili, chopped

Directions

1. First of all, preserve the pineapple, preserve a cup of chunks, half cup of juice.

2. Take half cup of juice and mix with meat, cilantro, ginger and soy sauce in bowl.

3. Allow to marinate, covered, for ¼ hour.

4. Fry the garlic in oil in sauté pan till fragrant.

5. Take the meat out of marinade and put in sauté pan.

6. Sauté and mix for FIVE min or till cooked through.

7. Take the meat out.

8. Mix the cornstarch and marinade in bowl.

9. Take marinade, pepper, beans, and chilies and add them to sauté pan.

10. Sauté and mix for FOUR min or till vegetables become soft and crunchy. And mixture become thick.

11. Blend in one cup of pineapple chunks.

12. Blend in meat.

13. Blend in scallions.

14. Heated through.

Steamed Halibut with Chili Lime Dressing

Ingredients

For the Dressing

- 3 limes, juice of
- 1 teaspoon kosher salt
- 1 tablespoon sugar
- 1 teaspoon oyster sauce
- 1 garlic clove, roughly chopped
- 1/2 teaspoon fresh ginger, roughly chopped
- 1/2 teaspoon chili sauce

For the Fish

- 1 lb. halibut fillet
- 3 roam tomatoes, sliced thinly
- 1 cucumber, thinly sliced
- 3 ounces fresh mint
- 1 tablespoon fresh Thai basil
- 1 tablespoon fresh cilantro
- 2 tablespoons fried shallots (optional)
- 1 tablespoon pickled red Chile (optional)

Directions

1. For preparing dressing;
2. Puree the items in food processor till smooth.
3. Adjust seasoning according to your own choice and taste.

For Fish;

1. **Put the tomato and cucumber on a dish.**
2. **Put the steamed fish over the tomato and cucumber.**
3. **Use the dressing to drizzle over fish.**
4. Chop the herbs and scatter over the fish.

BBQ Pork Spareribs

Ingredients

- 750 g pork spareribs
- 3 tablespoons soy sauce
- 3 tablespoons water
- 1 teaspoon sugar
- 1 tablespoon hoisin sauce
- 2 teaspoons gingerroot, shredded
- 2 teaspoons garlic, crushed
- 2 small onions, finely diced
- 3 tablespoons dry sherry
- 1/4 teaspoon ground black pepper
- 3 tablespoons chicken stock
- 1 tablespoon corn flour

Directions

1. First of all, blanch the ribs in boiling water for 120 seconds.

2. Take the soy sauce, water, sugar and mix them with diced onion, garlic, hoisin sauce and ginger in bowl.

3. Put the ribs into oiled baking tray and pour over sauce mixture.

4. Cook for 1/3 hour on low temperature setting.

5. Add the sherry. Add the pepper as seasoning and blend and turn over ribs.

6. Keep on cooking with hood down for next ¾ hour, mixing and turning the ribs a couple of times.

7. After this, turn the grill section of barbecue to high and shift the ribs to grill.

8. Cook for FIVE min per side or till crunchy and brown in color.

9. Take the chicken stock and mix with corn flour.

10. When the ribs are grilling, take chicken stock, corn flour and add them to sauce mixture.

11. Raise the temperature and blend well till sauce become thick.

12. You can serve this tasty and exotic recipe over the boiled rice.

13. Pour the sauce all over ribs.

Lemon Chicken and Asparagus Stir Fry

Ingredients

- 3 tablespoons reduced sodium soy sauce
- 3 tablespoons fresh lemon juice
- 1 teaspoon lemon zest, grated
- 1 teaspoon cornstarch
- 3/4 lb. boneless skinless chicken breast, cut in strips
- 1 tablespoon canola oil
- 2 garlic cloves, finely chopped
- 4 scallions, cut into 1-inch diagonal pieces
- 1/2 lb. asparagus, cut into diagonal pieces
- 1 carrot, julienned

Directions

1. Take the soy sauce and mix with cornstarch and lemon zest and lemon juice in a glass dish.

2. Add in the chicken.

3. Coat with marinade.

4. Allow to chill for ½ hour

5. Sauté the garlic in oil in sauté pan over moderately high temperature setting till tender.

6. Preserve marinade, add in chicken. Add in scallions.

7. Add in asparagus.

8. Add in carrot.

9. Sauté and mix for FOUR min or till pink color is gone from chicken.

10. Add in marinade.

11. Cook for 60 seconds till sauce become thick.

Mongolian Beef

Ingredients

- 1 tablespoon vegetable oil
- 1 garlic clove, finely minced
- 1 teaspoon chili sauce
- 1/2 cup soy sauce
- 1/3 cup sugar
- 1 lb. beef, sliced into bite-size pieces
- 1/2 cup sweet onion, shredded
- 1 teaspoon sesame oil

Directions

1. Fry the veggies and minced garlic in oil in skillet till become light golden in color.
2. Take chili sauce and mix with sugar and soy sauce in bowl.
3. Blend well and add to pan.
4. Add in beef into simmering sauce mixture in skillet.
5. Keep on simmering till liquid has been reduced.
6. After this, add in shredded onion. Add in dash of sesame oil
7. Sauté and mix till all of the items become soft and cooked.
8. You can serve this delicious recipe with rice.

Chicken Shish Kebab

Ingredients

- 4 chicken breasts, cut in chunks
- 1/4 cup sugar
- 1/2 cup soy sauce
- 1/3 cup oil
- 1/4 cup lemon juice
- 1/2 teaspoon garlic powder or 2 fresh garlic cloves, crushed
- Mushroom
- Green pepper, in chunks
- 1 large onion, in chunks
- Cherry tomatoes

Directions

1. Blend the items together and allow to marinate the chicken for 60 min.

2. After this, thread the vegetables onto skewers alternatively with the chicken.

3. Grill till chicken is cooked.

4. You can serve this delicious recipe with rice.

Chinese Salad Meals
Chinese Spring Roll Salad

Ingredients

Salad

- 2 ounces bean thread mug bean noodles
- 3 cups shredded Napa cabbage
- 1 cup torn watercress
- 1 carrot, cut into matchstick thin strips
- 1/2 cup seedless cucumber, cut into matchstick thin strips
- 1/2 cup red bell pepper, cut into matchstick thin strips
- 1 green onion, minced

- 1 cup chopped baby corn
- 2 tablespoons snipped cilantro
- 2 tablespoons snipped mint

Dressing

- 1 tablespoon sesame oil
- 2 tablespoons sweet chili sauce
- 2 tablespoons lime juice
- 1 teaspoon soy sauce
- 1 teaspoon minced gingerroot
- 1 large garlic clove, crushed
- 1/2 teaspoon lime zest
- Garnish with black sesame seed

Directions

1. First of all, take the bean threads and soak them in warm water for TEN min. drain them.
2. Cook them in boiling water for 120 seconds or till noodles like glasslike.
3. Drain them and rinse them and drain once again. Chop into lengths.
4. Put in bowl along with remaining salad items.
5. Whisk the dressing items in a small size bowl. Toss with salad.
6. Use the sesame seeds as garnish.

Sesame Tuna Salad

Ingredients

- 1/4 cup rice vinegar
- 3 tablespoons canola oil
- 2 tablespoons reduced-sodium soy sauce
- 1 tablespoon toasted sesame oil
- 1 1/2 teaspoons sugar
- 1 1/2 teaspoons minced fresh ginger
- 2 (6 ounce) cans water-packed chunk light tuna, drained
- 1 cup sliced sugar snap pea
- 2 scallions, sliced
- 6 cups thinly sliced Napa cabbage
- 4 radishes, sliced

- 1/4 cup fresh cilantro leaves
- 1 tablespoon sesame seeds
- Freshly ground pepper

Directions

1. Take ginger, sugar and whisk with sesame oil, vinegar, and canola oil and soy sauce in a bowl.
2. Take three tbsp. of dressing and mix with scallions, peas and tuna in moderate size bowl.
3. Distribute the cabbage into four dishes.
4. After this, mound ¼ of tuna mixture in the middle of each dish.
5. Use the radishes as garnish along with sesame seeds and cilantro.
6. Use the rest of dressing to drizzle all over.
7. Finally, season with pepper.

Peking Pork Pasta Salad

Ingredients

- 3/4 lb. lean pork, cut into 1/4-inch cubes
- 1 teaspoon vegetable oil
- 6 ounces small-shaped pasta, such as corkscrew, cooked and drained
- 1 lb. fresh spinach leaves, washed and drained

Dressing

- 4 tablespoons soy sauce
- 4 tablespoons sherry wine
- 1 tablespoon sesame oil

Garnishes

- Chopped scallion
- Sliced almonds

Directions

1. Blend the dressing.
2. Sauté and mix pork in oil in skillet over high temperature setting till slightly brown in color.
3. Take the pork strips and toss them with dressing.
4. Take pasta and toss with spinach.
5. Use the pork strips for topping.
6. Use the chopped green onion and slices of almond for garnish.

Fresh Lotus Root Salad

Ingredients

- 1 lb. fresh lotus root
- 1 1/2 tablespoons soy sauce
- 1 1/2 tablespoons white vinegar
- 1/2 tablespoon sesame oil
- 1/4 teaspoon Asian chili oil (optional)
- 2 tablespoons chopped cilantro
- Toasted black sesame seeds or sesame seeds

Directions

1. First of all, heat three quarts water to boiling in a pot.

2. Rinse the lotus roots.

3. After this, trim and remove the both ends of bulb. Don't forget to peel the skin.

4. Chop the root thick slices diagonal wise and place them in water with some of the vinegar.

5. After this, drain roots and place them in boiling.

6. Remove the pot from heat and cover the pot.

7. Allow to rest for FIVE min.

8. Drain and rinse.

9. Dry and place them in shallow bowl.

10. Take the soy sauce and mix with cilantro, chili oil, vinegar and sesame oil in bowl.

11. Take the dressing and pour this over the lotus roots and use the sesame seeds as garnish.

Pickled Radish Salad With Garlic

Ingredients

- 1 bunch red radish, about 48 radishes, trimmed of greenery and washed
- 2 tablespoons naturally fermented soy sauce
- 2 tablespoons rice wine or 1 tablespoon dry sherry
- 1 tablespoon chopped fresh coriander leaves
- 1 teaspoon dried garlic granules

Directions

1. Finely chop the radishes into slices. Add the rest of items. And blend them well.

2. Place radish pickle into a plate and scatter the rest of coriander leaves all over the top.

Oriental Spinach Salad

Ingredients

- 1 1/2 lbs. fresh baby spinach leaves
- 2 tablespoons sesame oil
- 1 teaspoon sugar
- 2 tablespoons rice wine vinegar
- 3 tablespoons soy sauce
- 1 teaspoon Dijon mustard
- 1 teaspoon toasted sesame seeds

Directions

1. Take spinach, wash it and dry it and put in bowl.

2. Take the sesame seeds, sesame oil and mix with mustard, soy sauce, vinegar and sugar.

3. After this, pour over the spinach.

4. Toss well.

5. Allow to rest for FIVE min. and toss once again properly well.

China Chicken Salad

Ingredients

- 4 chicken breast halves
- Olive oil
- Salt
- Fresh ground black pepper
- 1/2 lb. asparagus, ends removed, and cut in thirds diagonally
- 1 red bell pepper, cored and seeded and cut in strips about size of asparagus pieces
- 2 scallions, sliced diagonally (white and green parts)
- 1 tablespoon sesame seeds, toasted

For the dressing

- 1/2 cup vegetable oil
- 1/4 cup good apple cider vinegar
- 3 tablespoons soy sauce
- 1 1/2 tablespoons dark sesame oil
- 1/2 tablespoon honey
- 1 clove garlic, minced
- 1/2 teaspoon peeled grated fresh ginger
- 1/2 tablespoon sesame seeds, toasted
- 1/4 cup smooth peanut butter
- 2 teaspoons salt
- 1/2 teaspoon fresh ground black pepper

Directions

1. Put chicken breasts on a shallow pan and use the olive oil for rubbing the skin.

2. Use the salt and pepper as sprinkle.

3. Roast for approximately FORTY min at 35o degrees Fahrenheit or till chicken is ready and done.

4. Allow to cool for a while.

5. Remove the meat from bones and remove the skin and shred chicken into eatable pieces.

6. After this, blanch asparagus in pot of salted and boiling water for FIVE min or till soft and crunchy.

7. Put in ice water and drain well.

8. Take the chop chicken and mix with peppers and asparagus in bowl.

9. Whisk all of the dressing items and pour this over the veggies and chicken.

10. Add in scallions.

11. Add in sesame seeds.

12. Add the seasoning according to your own choice and taste.

Shallot-Soy Vinaigrette

Ingredients

- 1 cup grainy mustard
- 8 medium shallots, roughly chopped
- 1/4 cup Chinese black vinegar
- 1/2 cup naturally brewed rice wine vinegar
- 1/4 cup soy sauce
- 2 tablespoons sugar
- 2 cups grape seed oil or 2 cups canola oil
- Kosher salt
- Ground black pepper

Directions

1. Puree the sugar, soy sauce, mustard, vinegars, and shallots in blender.

2. After this, drizzle in oil till emulsified.

3. Add the salt and pepper.

Chinese Cabbage & Parsley Salad

Ingredients

- 4 cups Chinese cabbage, shredded
- 1 cup chopped pineapple
- 2 cups fresh parsley, roughly chopped
- 1 cup shredded carrot
- 1/2 red onion, thinly sliced
- 1/4 cup mayonnaise
- 4 tablespoons reserved pineapple juice
- 1 tablespoon whole grain mustard
- 1 tablespoon ginger, grated
- Salt & freshly ground black pepper, to taste

Directions

1. Take the finely sliced red onion, shredded carrot and mix with pineapple, cabbage and parsley in Ziploc bag.

2. Seal the bag and allow to chill.

3. Take the whole grain mustard, ginger and mix with mayonnaise, pineapple juice and salt and ground black pepper.

4. Cover and allow to cool.

5. Take the dressing and pour this into Ziploc bag and toss well.

Chinese Fruit Salad

Ingredients

- 2 tablespoons granulated sugar
- 1/4 teaspoon almond extract
- 1/4 teaspoon Chinese five spice powder
- 1 banana, peeled, sliced
- 1 cup mango, sliced (fresh or canned)
- 2 kiwi fruits, peeled, sliced
- 1 peach, pit removed, sliced thin
- 4 large strawberries, cut in half

Directions

1. Take the almond extra and mix with sugar and blend in 5spice powder and put aside.

2. After this, layer the slices of banana in ring shape in a bowl. Then lay the kiwi slices in the center.

3. Use little bit of sugar mixture as sprinkle all over.

4. Take mango slices and spread them over the bananas and kiwi.

5. Use more little bit of sugar mixture as sprinkle all over.

6. Then after this, lay peach slices around the dish and use sugar mixture as sprinkle.

7. Eventually, lay the strawberries in the center.

8. Use rest of sugar mixture as sprinkle all over the berries.

9. Allow to chill, covered.

Chinese Lunches and Snacks

Chinese Beef with Broccoli

Ingredients

- 1/2 kg beef sirloin tip, sliced thinly into strips
- 2 tablespoons cornstarch
- 1/4 cup rice wine
- 1/4 cup Kikkoman soy sauce
- 1 tablespoon sugar
- 2 green onions, cut into small pieces about 1/2 inch
- 1 head broccoli, cut diagonally across the stem
- 2 teaspoons oyster sauce

- 1 pinch baking soda
- 1/4 cup water, approx. just for it not to be dry and to have a little sauce
- 1 -2 tablespoon cooking oil

Directions

1. First of all, take the chopped meat strips and pound them with back of knife till become soft. And put aside.

2. Mix the rice wine and cornstarch.

3. Take meat and add to cornstarch and rice wine mixture.

4. Allow to marinate for a minimum of ½ hour.

5. After this, mix the sugar and Kikkoman soy sauce and put aside.

6. Chop the broccoli and chop the stems diagonally, remove the big stalk.

7. Sauté and mix the marinated beef in oil in sauté pan over moderate temperature, mixing till color is changed however only half done.

8. After this, take onions, Kikkoman and add them with sugar mixture.

9. After this, add broccoli.

10. Add in oyster sauce, keep on mixing for FIVE min or till cooked.

11. Add in pinch of soda as well to the broccoli.

12. After this, add in one fourth cup of water.

13. Sauté and mix for next 60 seconds.

Quick Hunan Grilled Chicken

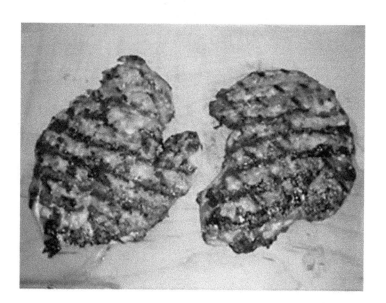

Ingredients

- 2 tablespoons hoisin sauce
- 1 tablespoon peanut butter
- 2 teaspoons soy sauce
- 1 clove garlic, minced
- 1 teaspoon hot pepper oil
- 1/8 teaspoon sesame oil
- 1 lb. boneless skinless chicken breast
- 4 leaves iceberg lettuce

Directions

1. First of all, pound the chicken breasts to half inch thickness.

2. Take the hoisin sauce, peanut butter and blend with oil and garlic.

3. After this, spread over on each side of chicken.

4. Grill the chicken for FIVE min each side or till cooked through.

5. Diagonally slice the chicken against the breast.

6. You can serve this chicken with iceberg lettuce piece

Szechuan Stir-Fried Beef

Ingredients

- 1 lb. boneless beef top sirloin steak, trimmed of fat
- 1/4 cup low sodium soy sauce
- 1/4 cup dry sherry
- 2 tablespoons water
- 2 teaspoons cornstarch
- 2 teaspoons fresh gingerroot, peeled and minced
- 1/2 teaspoon crushed red pepper flakes
- 1/2 teaspoon fresh ground black pepper
- 1 teaspoon chili powder
- 1 tablespoon vegetable oil
- 2 teaspoons minced garlic

Directions

1. Finely chop the steak into slices against the grain.
2. Mix the following 8 items together in a bowl till become smooth.
3. Sauté and mix the garlic and beef strips in oil in sauté pan for FOUR min or till cooked to moderate phase.
4. Blend in sauce.
5. Keep on mixing till sauce become thick and become bubbling.
6. You can serve this delicious recipe over the rice.

Szechuan Noodles

Ingredients

- 6 garlic cloves, chopped
- 1/4 cup fresh ginger, peeled and chopped
- 1/2 cup vegetable oil
- 1/2 cup tahini
- 1/2 cup smooth peanut butter
- 1/2 cup good soy sauce
- 1/4 cup dry sherry
- 1/4 cup sherry wine vinegar
- 1/4 cup honey
- 1/2 teaspoon hot chili oil
- 2 tablespoons dark sesame oil
- 1/2 teaspoon fresh ground black pepper
- 1/8 teaspoon ground cayenne pepper

- 1 lb. spaghetti
- 1 red bell pepper, julienned
- 1 yellow bell pepper, julienned
- 5 scallions, sliced diagonally

Directions

1. Put the ginger and garlic in blender.

2. Take veggie oil, ground peppers, sesame oil, chili oil, honey, tahini, peanut butter, soy sauce, sherry, sherry vinegar, honey and add them to blender.

3. After this, puree the sauce.

4. After this, add a splash of oil to pot of salted and boiling water.

5. Cook the spaghetti till ready and done, not tender.

6. Drain the pasta and put in bowl, toss with THREE FOURTH of sauce.

7. Add in red bell peppers. Then add in yellow bell peppers. Add in scallions. Toss them properly well.

Oriental Grilled Tuna

Ingredients

- 1/2 cup soy sauce
- 1 tablespoon honey
- 1/4 cup white wine
- 2 tablespoons Dijon mustard
- 4 (4 ounce) yellow-fin tuna steaks

Directions

1. Mix everything together besides tuna in a bowl.
2. Put tuna in mixture of sauce.
3. Allow to marinate for THREE hrs.
4. After this, grill the tuna over moderate temperature for TEN min or till cooked through, tuning one time.

Cantonese Chicken and Mushrooms

Ingredients

- 1 1/4 lbs. chicken tenders, cut into 1 1/2 inch pieces
- 1/2 cup oyster sauce
- 2 tablespoons cornstarch
- 2 tablespoons peanut oil
- 6 scallions, cut into 1 inch pieces
- 8 slices ginger (peeled and thinly sliced)
- 3 garlic cloves, coarsely chopped
- 8 -10 mushrooms, sliced (cremini, shitake or mixed)
- 12 ounces baby bok choy, cut crosswise into 1 1/2 inch pieces
- 1 1/4 cups low sodium chicken broth
- 2 teaspoons toasted sesame oil
- Cooked rice, for serving

Directions

1. Take the chicken and toss with oyster sauce in bowl.

2. Take cornstarch and blend with three tbsp. of cold water in separate bowl.

3. Put both of the bowls near to the stove with the rest of items.

4. Sauté and mix the scallions, garlic and ginger to peanut oil in sauté pan over high temperature setting for 1/3 min.

5. Add in chicken mixture and sauté mix till pink color is gone from meat on the outer side, for THREE min.

6. Blend in mushrooms.

7. Blend in bok choy.

8. After this, take broth, sesame oil and add them to sauté pan.

9. Heat to boiling over high temperature setting.

10. After this, add in cornstarch mixture and bring back to boil and cook, toss well, till chicken is cooked and sauce become thick.

11. You can serve this delicious recipe with rice.

Hot & Spicy Braised Prawns

Ingredients

- 1 lb. prawns, shelled and deveined
- 2 teaspoons sherry wine
- 2 teaspoons chili oil
- 3 cloves garlic, minced
- 3 teaspoons ginger, finely minced
- 3 green onions, minced
- 1 1/2 teaspoons sesame oil

Directions

1. Take oil, garlic and mix with ginger in skillet.
2. Sauté and mix for TEN seconds.
3. Add in sherry.
4. Add in soy sauce.
5. Add in chili oil.
6. Cook for 1.5 min.
7. After this, add in prawns.
8. Braise till become pink in color and look opaque for 1 min.
9. Add in green onion.
10. Cook for half min.

Hot and Spicy Szechuan Noodles

Ingredients

- 1/2 tablespoon Szechuan peppercorns
- 1 1/2 tablespoons peanut oil
- 1 teaspoon peanut oil, extra
- 8 ounces ground pork
- 2 cups chicken stock
- 1/2 cup Japanese pickled radishes, diced
- 4 tablespoons soy sauce
- 1 1/2 tablespoons black vinegar
- 1 tablespoon minced garlic
- 2 teaspoons sesame oil
- 1 teaspoon chili oil

- 1/4 teaspoon white pepper
- 1 lb. udon noodles or 1 lb. fresh wheat noodles
- 4 spring onions, finely sliced, for garnish

Directions

1. Dry fry peppercorns in sauté pan for THREE min.
2. Add in peanut oil.
3. Cook over low temperature setting for TEN min.
4. Allow to cool.
5. After this, strain oil into saucepan. Remove the peppercorns.
6. Take the chicken stock, white pepper, chili oil, sesame oil, garlic, preserved radish, soy sauce, black pepper AND add them to peppercorns oil in saucepan.
7. After this, heat over moderate temperature.
8. Cook the wheat noodles for TWO min in boiling water.
9. Drain well and add to mixture.
10. After this, sauté and mix the pork in additional oil in sauté pan over high temperature setting for FIVE min till crunchy and brown in color.
11. After this, distribute the noodle and broth mixture into soup bowls.
12. Use the pork for topping.
13. Use the spring onion as garnish.

Skillet Style Liver

Ingredients

- 1/2 lb. cooked white rice
- 1 red bell pepper, strips
- 1 sliced big head onion
- 2 tablespoons chopped coriander
- 1 cup mushroom, chopped into pieces
- 1 lb. beef liver, clean and cut into strips
- 1/2 on demi glace meat sauce dissolved in half cup cold water (Knorr)
- 4 tablespoons butter
- 2 tablespoons sesame
- 2 tablespoons soy sauce
- Salt

Directions

1. First of all, adobe liver with 2 tbsp. soy sauce.

2. Sauté the mushrooms, onions, and red bell peppers in butter for SEVEN min.

3. Take out of sauté pan.

4. Add to the same sauté pan over two tbsp. of butter.

5. And fry the liver.

6. Mix the veggies and add the coriander.

7. Add the demi glace meat sauce and boil to low temperature till sauce become thick.

8. You can serve this delicious recipe over the cradle of rice. Use the sesame for decoration.

Chinese Baked Eggs

Ingredients

- 4 ounces fresh shrimp, shelled and deveined
- 5 eggs
- 1/2 cup chicken stock
- 1 teaspoon salt
- 2 tablespoons peanut oil
- 1 tablespoon sherry wine

Directions

1. Dry the washed shrimp completely and chop finely.

2. After this, beat the eggs.

3. Add in stock. Add in shrimp. Add in salt. Add in oil and add in sherry and blend well.

4. Take the mixture and pour this into sprayed casserole dish.

5. Bake for ¼ hour at FOUR HUNDRED (4oo) degrees Fahrenheit.

Eggs with Crab Meat

Ingredients

- 1/2 lb. fresh crabmeat, flaked
- 6 eggs
- 1 cup chicken stock
- 2 tablespoons light soy sauce
- 3 tablespoons oil
- 1 tablespoon fresh ginger, chopped fine
- 2 scallions, chopped fine
- 1 tablespoon cornstarch, dissolved in 2 T. water
- 1 tablespoon red wine vinegar
- Hot steamed rice

Directions

1. Take crab meat and mix with stock and eggs.

2. After this, add in soy sauce and beat well.

3. Sauté and mix the scallion and ginger in one tablespoon of oil in sauté pan over moderately low temperature setting for 60 seconds.

4. Take out and put aside.

5. After this, sauté and mix the crab meat and egg mixture in two tablespoons of oil in sauté pan over moderately high temperature setting.

6. Once the mixture begins to set, add in ginger. Add in scallion.

7. Sauté for next 120 seconds.

8. If you want to thicken it, add dissolved cornstarch.

9. Blend in vinegar.

10. You can serve this delicious recipe over the steamed rice.

Chinese-style Rice Paper Rolls

Ingredients

- 1 small cucumber, peeled and julienned
- 1 small carrot, peel and julienned
- 1/4 cup mint leaf
- 3 tablespoons pickled ginger, finely sliced (optional)
- 40 g baby dou miao or 40 g snow pea sprouts
- 1 bunch chives, cut in 9 cm lengths
- 10 g enoki mushrooms
- Rice paper sheet
- DIPPING SAUCE INGREDIENTS
- 3 tablespoons freshly squeezed lime juice
- 3 tablespoons Thai fish sauce

- 1 clove garlic, crushed
- 2 small red chilies, finely sliced
- 1 tablespoon brown sugar or 1 tablespoon palm sugar

Directions

1. First of all, soak the rice paper sheets in warm water to soften them.

2. After this, take out and put on a cotton cloth.

3. Lay small quantity of filling along the middle top of rice paper.

4. After this, fold one side towards middle and then after this, fold the bottom up towards top.

5. After this, roll wrap over towards the rest of side for making a roll.

6. Do the same process till rice and filling are finished.

7. Mix the dipping sauce items in bowl.

8. You can serve this delicious sauce recipe with rice paper rolls.

Delicious Szechuan Nuts

Ingredients

- 2 teaspoons five-spice seasoning
- 1 teaspoon salt
- 1 tablespoon water
- 2 cups raw nuts, any variety
- 1 teaspoon sesame oil

Directions

1. Blend the spice seasoning, water and salt. And then after this, add to nuts. Blend well prior to adding oil.

2. After this, blend in oil. Toss well prior to spreading on a dish.

3. Cook for THREE min on high temperature setting.

4. Blend well and leave the center open.

5. Cook for next FIVE min on high temperature setting.

6. Allow to cool.

Szechuan Peppercorn Chicken

Ingredients

- 2 teaspoons Szechuan peppercorns
- 2 tablespoons scallions, chopped
- 2 teaspoons fresh ginger, finely chopped
- 1/2 teaspoon salt
- 3 tablespoons soy sauce
- 2 tablespoons sesame oil
- 1 tablespoon chicken stock
- 1 teaspoon red wine vinegar
- 1 teaspoon sugar
- 1 head iceberg lettuce, shredded
- 1 1/2 lbs. cooked shredded chicken

Directions

1. First of all, take out seeds from peppercorns and remove the seeds and crush peppercorns.

2. Blend the rest of items.

3. Put the lettuce on a dish and organize the chicken over it.

4. After this, pour over the sauce.

Chinese One Dishes

Chili Crusted Chicken Noodles

Ingredients

- 3 teaspoons chili powder
- 6 tablespoons corn flour
- 3 teaspoons salt
- 2 -4 tablespoons peanut oil
- 2 chicken breasts, sliced
- 4 spring onions, sliced
- 1 carrot, thinly sliced for stir frying
- 2 tablespoons mirin or 2 tablespoons sherry wine
- 2 (500 g) packages hokkien noodles
- 2 tablespoons oyster sauce

Directions

1. Take the chili powder and mix with salt and corn flour and then coat the chicken slices.
2. Cook the chicken in peanut oil in sauté pan over moderately high temperature setting.
3. Take out of sauté pan and drain on paper towels.
4. Place the hokkein noodles in strainer and run under water for separating the noodles.
5. Heat the sauté pan again over moderate temperature.
6. After this, add a splash of oil and sauté and mix the carrot and spring onion for 60 seconds.
7. After this, add in mirin. Add in noodles. Toss for 60 seconds.
8. After this, add in oyster sauce.
9. Add in two tab water.
10. Blend through.
11. Allow to steam, covered, for THREE min.
12. After this, toss in chicken and steam, covered, for ½ min.

Spicy Szechuan Beef

Ingredients

- 1/2 lb. round steak, cut into thin slivers
- 7 tablespoons soy sauce, divided
- 2 tablespoons sugar, divided
- 1/2 teaspoon white pepper
- 3 tablespoons cornstarch
- 4 tablespoons oil, divided
- 3 tablespoons hoisin sauce
- 1 -2 teaspoon cayenne, to taste
- 2 cups celery, julienned
- 1 cup carrot, julienned
- 2 green onions, julienned
- Serve with
- Steamed white rice

Directions

1. Take four tbsp. of soy sauce and mix with two tbsp. of oil, white pepper, cornstarch, one tbsp. of sugar for making marinade.

2. After this, add in beef.

3. Allow to rest for ½ hour.

4. Take three tbsp. of soy sauce, cayenne and mix with one tbsp. of sugar, cayenne and hoisin sauce. Preserve.

5. After this, sauté and mix the beef in rest of oil in sauté pan over high temperature setting for THREE min.

6. After this, add the veggies to meat. Sauté and mix till ready and done, crunchy and soft.

7. After this, add in prepared sauce.

8. Cook for ½ min or heated through.

Chicken Stir-Fry

Ingredients

- 1 lb. boneless skinless chicken breast (cut into strips)
- 1 cup salad dressing
- 1 package frozen mixed vegetables or 1 package assorted fresh vegetable, cut up
- 2 tablespoons soy sauce
- 1 teaspoon garlic powder
- 1 cup peanuts or 1 dozen cashews
- 2 cups Minute Rice

Directions

1. First of all, cook the chopped chicken breast strips in salad dressing in sauté pan on moderately high temperature for THREE min or till ready and done.

2. After this, add in veggies.

3. Blend in soy sauce.

4. Blend in garlic powder.

5. Keep on cooking for FIVE min or till chicken cooked through.

6. Add in peanuts and use the stir-fry as sprinkle.

7. Then cook the minute rice as instructed on the package.

8. You can serve this delicious recipe over the noodles.

Sweet and Sour Ramen Chicken

Ingredients

- 1 cup bell pepper, chopped
- 1/2 teaspoon ginger
- 4 whole green onions, thinly sliced
- 1 (20 ounce) cans pineapple chunks in juice, untrained
- 1 lb. boneless chicken breast
- Oil
- 2 (3 ounce) packages chicken-flavored ramen noodles
- 1/2 cup sweet and sour sauce

Directions

1. First of all, drain pineapple juice in a cup and add water to measure two cups and put aside.

2. After this, chop the chicken into pieces and use ginger for seasoning.

3. Sauté and mix the chicken in little bit of oil for FOUR min.

4. After this, add in pineapple juice.

5. Heat to boiling.

6. Break the noodles and add to sauté pan along with seasoning packets.

7. Heat back to boiling, lower the temperature and allow to simmer for THREE min or till noodles become soft and majority of the liquid has been assimilated.

8. After this, add in sweet and sour sauce.

9. Add in pepper.

10. Add in onion.

11. Add in pineapple.

12. Cook till peppers become crunchy and soft.

Spicy Mongolian Beef

Ingredients

- 1/2 tablespoon cornstarch
- 1 tablespoon rice vinegar
- 1/2 cup dark soy sauce
- 1 tablespoon black bean sauce
- 1 tablespoon sesame oil
- 2 teaspoons sambal oelek
- 500 g flank steaks, finely sliced
- 1 teaspoon five-spice powder
- 1 teaspoon sugar
- 2 garlic cloves, minced
- 1 egg, lightly beaten

- 1 medium brown onion, finely chopped
- 1 head broccoli, cut into florets
- 1 medium carrot, finely chopped
- 1 red bell pepper, finely chopped
- 10 snow peas, chopped in half
- 1/3 cup beef stock or 1/3 cup vegetable stock or 1/3 cup water

Directions

1. Take cornstarch and mix with vinegar and half sauces.
2. Then allow to marinate the beef in five spices, garlic, sugar, and egg and sauce mixture for 60 min.
3. Sauté and mix beef in half of oil in sauté pan. Put the cooked beef aside.
4. Sauté and mix the onion in rest of oil in sauté pan till become tender.
5. Add in carrot.
6. Add in bell pepper.
7. Cook for next 60 seconds.
8. Bring the beef back to sauté pan along with snow peas and broccoli.
9. Add in the preserved marinade. Add in remaining sauces. Add in stock.
10. Cook, mixing from time to time till sauces boils and become slightly thick.
11. You can serve this delicious recipe with rice.

Noodles with Stir-Fried Tofu and Broccoli

Ingredients

- 1 lb. firm tofu
- 8 ounces soba noodles or 8 ounces Chinese wheat noodles or 8 ounces linguine
- 1 tablespoon canola oil
- 2 large broccoli florets, cut into bite size pieces
- 1/3 cup stir-fry sauce

Directions

1. Chop the tofu into slices.

2. Dry them and chop them into half inch dice.

3. Cook the noodles as instructed on the box. And then drain well.

4. Sauté and mix the tofu in oil in sauté pan over moderately high temperature setting till golden in color.

5. Take out of pan.

6. Take the broccoli and mix with ONE FOURTH cup of water in sauté pan.

7. Allow to steam, covered, till crunchy and soft.

8. Add in tofu.

9. Add in cooked noodles.

10. Sauté and mix the sauce to pan.

11. Toss well.

12. Cook till ready and done.

Chinatown Chicken Salad

Ingredients

- Nonstick cooking spray
- 8 (6 1/2 inch) wonton wrappers
- 2 cups cooked chicken breasts, shredded
- 4 cups iceberg lettuce or 4 cups romaine lettuce, shredded
- 1/2 lb. bean sprouts
- 3 green onions, sliced
- 1/4 cup cilantro leaf, chopped
- 1/4 cup coarsely chopped salted peanuts
- Dressing
- 1/4 cup plum sauce
- 2 tablespoons rice wine vinegar
- 2 teaspoons sesame oil
- 1/2 teaspoon dry mustard

Directions

1. First of all, use the oil for greasing the foil tart pans.

2. Chop the wrappers into circular shapes.

3. Fit each one into pans.

4. Then grease each of the wrapper.

5. Bake for SEVEN min at THREE SEVENTY FIVE (375) degrees Fahrenheit or till golden brown in color.

6. Take out and allow to cool.

7. Keep in airtight container.

8. Take the bean sprouts, lettuce, and mix with chicken, cilantro and onions in bowl.

9. Whisk the dressing items in bowl.

10. Take dressing and pour this over the salad and toss well.

11. After this, spoon a cup into every shell.

12. Use the peanuts as sprinkle.

Szechuan Noodle Toss

Ingredients

- 1 (8 ounce) packages thin spaghetti
- 1/4 cup sesame oil, divided
- 2 large red bell peppers, cut into julienne strips
- 4 green onions, cut into 1 inch pieces
- 2 cloves garlic, minced
- 1 (10 ounce) bags fresh spinach, torn into bite-size pieces
- 2 cups cubed cooked chicken
- 1 (8 ounce) cans sliced water chestnuts, drained
- 1/4 cup soy sauce
- 2 tablespoons rice vinegar
- 1 1/2 teaspoons crushed red pepper flakes
- 1 -2 teaspoon minced fresh gingerroot

Directions

1. First of all, prepare the spaghetti as instructed on the package and drain and rinse and then drain once again.

2. Place the spaghetti in bowl and put aside.

3. Sauté and mix the red pepper strips, garlic and green onions for 120 seconds in two tbsp. of sesame oil in sauté pan.

4. Mix in spinach. Cook, covered, and over moderate temperature setting for THREE min or till spinach wilts.

5. Take the sauté pan away from heat and allow to cool.

6. Take the spinach mixture and spoon this over the spaghetti.

7. After this, add water chestnuts. Then add chicken.

8. Take two tbsp. of sesame oil, and mix with rest of items in bowl and blend well.

9. After this, pour over the pasta and toss well.

Chinese Steamed Fish

Ingredients

- 4 (4 -6 ounce) fish fillets
- 2 tablespoons mirin
- 1/4 teaspoon granulated sugar (to taste)
- 1/4 teaspoon salt
- 2 -3 drops sesame oil
- 1 green onion, finely chopped
- 1 tablespoon cilantro, chopped
- 1 large lemon, cut into wedges

Directions

1. First of all, rinse the fish fillet and dry them.

2. Take the rice wine, and whisk with sesame oil and salt and sugar in bowl.

3. Put the fish fillets on a dish.

4. Take the rice wine mixture and pour this over fish.

5. Use the chopped green onion as sprinkle.

6. Allow to steam, covered, the fish over high temperature setting till fish flakes easy, approximately ¼ hour.

7. Use the chopped cilantro along with lemon wedges as garnishes.

Egg Foo Yung

Ingredients

- 3 eggs, beaten
- Salt and pepper
- Five-spice powder, a good pinch (optional)
- 3 tablespoons sunflower oil
- 4 green onions, sliced
- 1 clove garlic, crushed
- 1 small green pepper, seeded and chopped
- 4 ounces fresh bean sprouts
- 3 cups cooked jasmine rice
- 3 tablespoons light soy sauce
- 1 tablespoon sesame oil

Directions

1. First of all, take eggs and season them and beat in 5 spice powder.
2. Pour in egg in a tbsp. of oil in skillet.
3. Cook the egg till become firm. And after this, tip out.
4. Cut into strips.
5. Sauté and mix the garlic, pepper, and bean sprouts in rest of oil for 120 seconds, mixing and tossing constantly.
6. Blend in cooked rice and heated completely, mix well.
7. After this, add in soy sauce.
8. Add in sesame oil.
9. Bring the egg back and blend in well.

Chicken, Spring Onion and Noodle Stir Fry

Ingredients

- 2 boneless skinless chicken breasts, cut into strips
- 1 tablespoon olive oil
- 2 blocks thin egg noodles
- 1 tablespoon fresh ginger, grated
- 1 -2 garlic clove, minced
- 6 -10 spring onions, sliced into half inch pieces
- 3 tablespoons light soy sauce
- 200 ml chicken stock
- 1 pinch black pepper

Directions

1. Cook the noodles as instructed on the packet and then drain them.
2. Sauté the ginger and garlic in oil in pan, mixing for ½ min.
3. Add in chicken. And mix around pan.
4. Prepare the stock. Take soy sauce and add to stock. Blend well.
5. Look for the chicken whether cooked or not, prior to moving on.
6. After this, add in spring onions and mix for short period of time.
7. Blend in stock.
8. Add in noodles.
9. Blend all of the items.
10. Add in pinch of black pepper and toss well.

Chinese Beef Curry Stir-Fry

Ingredients

- 3 tablespoons soy sauce
- 1 tablespoon minced garlic
- 1 tablespoon minced fresh gingerroot or 1 teaspoon ground ginger
- 4 tablespoons oil, divided
- 1 lb. boneless sirloin steak, cut into thin strips
- 1 onion, cut into pieces
- 1 green pepper, cut into strips
- 1 red pepper, cut into strips
- 2 celery ribs, thinly sliced
- 1 cup water
- 5 teaspoons cornstarch
- 1 1/2 teaspoons curry powder

Directions

1. Take the soy sauce and mix with two tablespoon of oil, ginger and garlic.

2. After this, add the beef and toss well.

3. Allow to chill for ¼ hour.

4. Sauté and mix the beef in rest of oil in sauté pan over moderate temperature setting for 120 seconds.

5. Take out beef and put aside.

6. Sauté and mix the onion for 60 seconds.

7. Add in celery. Add in peppers. Sauté and mix for 120 seconds.

8. Bring the beef back to sauté pan.

9. Take the cornstarch and mix with curry and water till become smooth.

10. Add to sauté pan, heat to boiling, mixing continuously.

11. Boil for 60 seconds.

Honey Lime Cajun Shrimp Stir Fry

Ingredients

- Marinade
- 1/3 cup lime juice
- 1/3 cup honey
- 2 teaspoons light soy sauce
- 2 tablespoons Cajun seasoning
- Salt and pepper (optional)
- Stir Fry
- 1 lb. raw shrimp, peeled and deveined
- 1 sweet potato, peeled and cubed
- 2 carrots, peeled and cut into rounds
- 1/2 lb. sugar snap pea, ends trimmed and cut in half if large

- 2 cups shredded cabbage
- 1 red onion, cut into wedges and layers separated
- 1 tablespoon cornstarch
- 1/4 cup cold water
- 2 cups cooked brown rice

Directions

1. Blend the marinade items in bowl.
2. Put the shrimp in sealable container and pour ½ of marinade all over them.
3. Keep in refrigerator for 60 min.
4. Pour the preserved marinade into sauté pan on high temperature setting.
5. Add the veggies to sauté pan and cook, mixing from time to time, for TEN min, or till veggies become soft.
6. Move the veggies to a side of sauté pan and add in shrimp.
7. Cook, mixing often, till shrimp become pink in color.
8. Take the cornstarch and mix with ONE FOURTH cup water and then add to sauté pan to thicken sauce.
9. Cook for approximately 60 seconds.

Chinese Pork Fried Rice

Ingredients

- 2 tablespoons oil
- 1 cup sliced mushrooms
- 1 cup bean sprouts
- 3 cups cold cooked rice
- 1 cup cold cooked pork, small dice
- 2 green onions with tops, sliced
- 3 eggs, lightly beaten
- 1 tablespoon oil
- 3 tablespoons soy sauce
- 1/4 teaspoon pepper

Directions

1. Fry the mushrooms in oil in sauté pan for 120 seconds.
2. Add in bean sprouts. Add in rice. Add in pork. Add in onion.
3. Sauté and mix for SIX min.
4. Move the rice to one side. Add one tablespoon of oil.
5. Add in eggs and cook and mix till eggs become thick.
6. Take eggs and mix with rice together.
7. Blend in pepper. Blend in soy sauce.
8. Serve.

Chinese Dessert Meals

Chinese Peanut Butter Fudge

Ingredients

- 1/2 cup butter
- 2 1/4 cups brown sugar
- 1/2 cup milk
- 3/4 cup peanut butter
- 1 teaspoon vanilla extract
- 3 1/2 cups confectioners' sugar

Directions

1. Melt the butter in saucepan over moderate temperature setting.
2. Mix in milk. Mix in brown sugar.
3. Boil for 120 seconds, mixing from time to time.
4. Take away from heat.
5. Blend in peanut butter.
6. Blend in vanilla.
7. Put the confectioners' sugar in bowl.
8. Pour the peanut butter mixture all over the sugar and beat well till become smooth.
9. After this, pour the fudge into pan. And allow to chill for 60 min.
10. Then chop in square shapes.

Coconut Oatmeal Cookies

Ingredients

- 1/2 cup shortening
- 1 cup brown sugar, packed or 2 tablespoons molasses
- 1 cup white sugar
- 2 large eggs
- 1 teaspoon vanilla
- 1/2 cup butter
- 2 cups flour
- 1 cup flaked coconut
- 1 teaspoon baking powder
- 1 teaspoon baking soda
- 2 cups rolled oats
- 1 cup raisins (optional) or 1 cup chocolate chips (optional)

Directions

1. Mix the butter, sugars and shortening in a bowl.
2. Mix in eggs. Mix in vanilla. Put aside.
3. Mix the dry items in another bowl.
4. Once all the items are mixed, add in coconut.
5. Mix the dry and wet items.
6. Drop onto cookie sheet that has been sprayed.
7. Bake for TEN min at 35o degrees Fahrenheit or till become golden brown in color.

Fresh Peach Cobbler

Ingredients

- 3 cups peaches, peeled, pitted and sliced
- 1 1/2 cups sugar, divided
- 1 cup flour
- 1 teaspoon baking powder
- 1/4 teaspoon salt
- 1/2 cup margarine
- 1/2 teaspoon vanilla
- 1/2 cup milk
- 1/2 cup water

Directions

1. First of all, spray the pan and use the peaches for lining the pan.

2. Take half cup of sugar, milk, vanilla and mix with margarine, salt, flour, and baking powder.

3. Blend well till become smooth.

4. After this, pour this over the peaches.

5. Mix water and a cup of sugar. And pour over the batter.

6. Bake for 60min at THREE FIFTY (35o) degrees Fahrenheit.

Chinese Strawberry Pie

Ingredients

- 1 pie crust, pre-baked
- 1 pint ripe strawberry
- 1 (3 ounce) packages strawberry Jell-O gelatin dessert
- 2 tablespoons cornstarch
- 1 cup hot water
- 1 cup cold water
- 1/2 cup sugar
- Whipped cream

Directions

1. First of all, pre bake the pie crust and allow to cool.

2. Chop the strawberries into pie crust.

3. Take package of jello and mix with cornstarch in saucepan.

4. Add in water. Add in sugar.

5. Cook over moderate temperature setting till boiling.

6. Mixing from time to time.

7. Take the boiling mixture and pour this over strawberries.

8. Let the pie chill in refrigerator for FOUR hrs.

9. You can serve this delicious dessert with dollops of whipped cream all over.

Chinese Pumpkin Pie

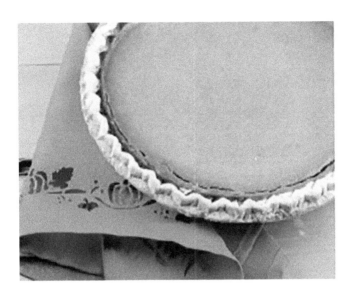

Ingredients

- 1 3/4 cups canned pumpkin
- 1 3/4 cups sweetened condensed milk
- 2 large eggs, beaten
- 2/3 cup firmly packed light brown sugar
- 2 tablespoons sugar
- 1 1/4 teaspoons ground cinnamon
- 1/2 teaspoon salt
- 1/2 teaspoon ground ginger
- 1/2 teaspoon ground nutmeg
- 1/4 teaspoon ground cloves
- 1 (9 inch) pie crusts, unbaked

Directions

1. Take the pumpkin and mix with the rest of items in bowl and beat at moderate speed setting for 120 seconds.

2. After this, pour into pie-crust.

3. Bake for ¼ hour at FOUR TWENTY FIVE (425) degrees Fahrenheit.

4. Lower the temperature to 35o and bake for next ¾ hour or till knife comes out neat and clean when inserted in the middle.

5. Allow to cool.

Blueberry Boy Bait

Ingredients

- 2 cups flour
- 1 1/2 cups sugar
- 2/3 cup butter
- 2 teaspoons baking powder
- 1 teaspoon salt
- 1 cup milk
- 2 eggs, separated
- 1 teaspoon vanilla
- 2 cups blueberries

Directions

1. Take butter, sugar and blend with flour.

2. Preserve ¾ cup of the mixture.

3. Take the baking powder, milk, egg yolks, and salt and add them to rest of mixture.

4. Mix well.

5. After this, beat the egg whites and fold into batter and pour this into baking pan.

6. Use the blueberries as sprinkle all over.

7. Use the preserved mixture for topping.

8. Bake for approximately ¾ hour at THREE FIFTY (35o) degrees Fahrenheit.

Cake Batter Ice Cream

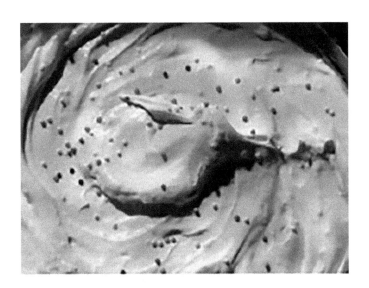

Ingredients

- 1 cup whole milk, well chilled
- 3/4 cup granulated sugar
- 2 cups heavy cream, well chilled
- 1 teaspoon pure vanilla extract
- 2/3 cup cake mix

Directions

1. First of all, put ice cream maker bowl into freezer.
2. Take the milk, and whisk with granulated sugar in bowl till sugar dissolves.
3. Blend in heavy creamy. Blend in vanilla.
4. Mix in cake mix till lumps are disappeared.
5. Take mixture and pour this into freezer bowl and allow to blend till become thick, approximately ½ hour.
6. Take out ice cream from freezer bowl and put in another container.
7. Take the freezer bowl, ice cream and put them into freezer.

Zucchini Chocolate Cake

Ingredients

- 1/2 cup butter
- 1/2 cup vegetable oil
- 1 3/4 cups sugar
- 2 large eggs
- 1/2 cup buttermilk or 1/2 cup sour milk
- 1 teaspoon vanilla
- 1/4 cup cocoa
- 2 1/2 cups flour
- 1 teaspoon baking soda
- 1 teaspoon salt
- 2 cups zucchini, grated
- 3/4 cup chocolate chips
- 1/2 cup walnuts

Directions

1. Mix the butter and add in oil. Then add in sugar mix.

2. Add the following eight items and blend them.

3. After this, fold in chips.

4. Fold in nuts.

5. Place into pan that has been sprayed and floured.

6. Bake for 60 min at THREE TWENTY FIVE (325) degrees Fahrenheit.

Chinese Custard Tarts

Ingredients

- 3 cups plain flour
- 185 g lard
- 5 tablespoons hot water
- 1 pinch salt
- **Custard**
- 3 eggs
- 1/3 cup sugar
- 1 1/2 cups milk
- 3 drops yellow food coloring

Directions

1. For preparing pastry, take flour and sift with salt in bowl.
2. After this, rub the lard into flour till mixture look like fine breadcrumbs.
3. Blend in hot water for make firm dough.
4. Knead on floured surface.
5. Roll out and chop out with fluted cutter and place into sprayed patty tins.
6. Take eggs and beat with sugar. Blend in milk. Blend in food coloring and blend them.
7. Pour the custard into pastry cases.
8. Bake for TEN min at FOUR SEVENTY FIVE (475) degrees Fahrenheit, lower the temperature to 425 and cook for next ¼ hour.

Chinese Walnut Cookies

Ingredients

- 1 cup unsalted butter, room temperature
- 1 cup powdered sugar
- 2 cups all-purpose flour
- 1 teaspoon baking powder
- 1/3 cup walnuts, chopped
- 1/4 cup dry roasted salted peanut, chopped
- 2 tablespoons eggs, beaten

Directions

1. Use a baking sheet for layering on baking pan.
2. Take butter, powdered sugar and mix with all purpose flour and baking powder.
3. Blend well and form dough.
4. Keep in refrigerator, covered, for 1/3 hour.
5. Take peanut, walnut and add them to bowl.
6. After this, fold the nuts into dough.
7. Distribute into nine pieces and roll out each one into a ball shape.
8. After this, press every dough for making a little flat.
9. Shift dough to baking pan.
10. Brush the dough surface with beaten egg.
11. Bake till become golden brown in color.
12. Allow the cookies to set on baking pan for FIVE min.
13. Then shift them to wire rack and allow to cool.

Chinese Soup Meals

Potato Sausage Soup

Ingredients

- 1 lb. low-fat breakfast sausage
- 5 -6 cups russet potatoes (peeled and chopped)
- 2 (14 ounce) cans chicken broth
- 3/4 cup sweet onion (chopped)
- 1 (12 ounce) cans evaporated milk
- Garlic powder
- Cracked pepper
- 2 cups 2% cheddar cheese (shredded)

Directions

1. Cook the onion and sausage in Dutch oven till pink color is gone.
2. Take chicken broth and add to sausage and onions.
3. Heat to boiling.
4. Add in potatoes.
5. Allow to simmer for 1/3 hour on moderately high temperature setting or till tender.
6. Take away from heat. And mash the potatoes.
7. Blend in evaporated milk.
8. Blend in cheese till melted.
9. Add in garlic powder.
10. Add in cracked pepper.

Chinese Egg Drop Soup

Ingredients

- 4 cups chicken broth
- 1 teaspoon soy sauce
- 1 teaspoon cornstarch, mixed with 2 t water
- 2 eggs, lightly beaten
- 2 green onions, chopped (the whole onion)
- Salt and pepper

Directions

1. Heat the soy sauce and broth to boiling.
2. Add in cornstarch mix, mixing till become thick.
3. Lower to simmer.
4. Add in eggs. Mixing.
5. Turn down the heat and add in onion. Add in salt. Add in pepper.

Chinese Soup with Tofu

Ingredients

- 1 tablespoon oil
- 2 medium carrots, cut into matchstick
- 1 medium onion, chopped
- 2 teaspoons ginger, grated
- 2 garlic cloves, minced
- 6 cups water
- 1/4 cup soy sauce
- 2 teaspoons rice vinegar
- 2 teaspoons sesame oil
- 1/2 teaspoon black pepper
- 12 ounces firm tofu
- 2 cups bok choy, chopped
- 2 cups Chinese cabbage, chopped
- 1 cup snow peas, cut in half

Directions

1. Fry the garlic, ginger, carrots and onion in pan in oil till onion become soft.

2. Add in water. Add in soy sauce. Add in pepper. Add in sesame oil. Add in rice vinegar.

3. Heat to boiling.

4. Lower the temperature to simmer for ¼ hour, mixing from time to time.

5. After this, prepare the tofu and remove additional water and chop the tofu into 3 slabs.

6. Sauté in oil till both of the sides become brown in color.

7. Drain well. Chop the tofu slabs into cubes.

8. After this, add the tofu cubes. Add in bok choy. Add in cabbage. Add in snow peas.

9. Allow to simmer for TEN min.

Chicken and Snow Pea Noodle Bowl

Ingredients

- 5 cups chicken broth
- 4 ounces uncooked vermicelli, broken into thirds
- 1/2 lb. cooked chicken, cubed
- 3 ounces snow peas (fresh or frozen)
- 1 cup matchstick cut carrot (or shredded)
- 1/2 teaspoon chili sauce
- 1/2 cup chopped green onion
- 1/4 cup chopped cilantro
- 2 tablespoons lime juice
- 2 teaspoons soy sauce
- 1 tablespoon grated ginger

Directions

1. First of all, heat the broth to boiling in saucepan over high temperature setting.

2. Blend in vermicelli.

3. Bring back to boiling.

4. Lower the temperature to moderately high.

5. Allow to simmer for SIX min.

6. Blend in chicken. Blend in snow peas. Blend in chili sauce. Blend in carrots.

7. Allow to simmer for 120 seconds.

8. Take away from heat. And blend in green onions. Blend in cilantro.

9. Blend in ginger. Blend in soy sauce and blend in lime juice.

Chicken and Sweetcorn Soup

Ingredients

- 1 (15 ounce) cans cream-style corn
- 500 ml water
- 1/2 chicken stock cube, dissolved in small amount water
- 200 -300 g skinless chicken pieces
- 2 eggs, beaten
- 3 spring onions, finely sliced
- Salt
- Pepper

Directions

1. First of all, boil the water. Add in creamed style corn.
2. Add in dissolved chicken stock.
3. Blend well.
4. When boiled, add in chicken pieces.
5. Allow to simmer for FIVE min.
6. Heat back to boiling.
7. Remove the soup from heat and allow to cool for a couple of seconds.
8. Add the beaten egg, mixing.
9. After this, add salt as well as pepper according to your own choice.
10. Use the spring onions as sprinkle.

Mustard Green and Sweet Potato Soup

Ingredients

- 1 lb. broad leaf mustard greens
- 1 large sweet potato
- 6 cups water

Directions

1. First of all, wash the mustard greens.
2. Chop them into pieces.
3. Chop the peeled sweet potato into chunks.
4. Heat all of the items to boiling, lower the temperature.
5. Allow to simmer, covered, for 180 min.

Egg Flower Soup

Ingredients

- 14 ounces plum tomatoes, 1 can
- 1 tablespoon light soy sauce
- 1 pint chicken stock
- 1 egg, lightly beaten
- 2 spring onions, chopped finely

Directions

1. First of all, chopped the drained tomatoes and preserve the juice.
2. Heat the stock, soy sauce, and tomato juice to boiling.
3. After this, add in tomatoes.
4. Add in half of the spring onions.
5. Cook for 120 seconds.
6. After this, slowly dribble in beaten eggs.
7. Use the rest of spring onions as sprinkle.

Delicious Jade Soup

Ingredients

- 1 whole boneless skinless chicken breast
- 4 1/2 cups chicken stock
- 2 egg whites
- 1 tablespoon cornstarch
- 2 teaspoons salt
- 4 ounces spinach leaves
- 2 tablespoons oil
- 1 tablespoon sherry wine
- 2 tablespoons cornstarch, dissolved in
- 2 tablespoons cold water

Directions

1. Finely chop the chicken and soak in ½ c of chicken stock.
2. After this, beat the egg whites and fold the cornstarch.
3. Then fold in chicken.
4. Fold in one teaspoon of salt. Put aside.
5. After this, cook the spinach in small quantity of boiling water.
6. Drain properly well and finely chop.
7. Sauté and mix the spinach in oil over moderately high temperature setting for ½ min.
8. Take the rest of 4c chicken stock, sherry and pour them over the spinach and heat to boiling.
9. Heat to boiling.
10. After this, add in chicken mixture and heat to boiling, mixing quickly.
11. Add one teaspoon of salt.
12. Add in the dissolved cornstarch if want it thick.

3 Delicious Pearls Soup

Ingredients

- 4 ounces chicken breasts
- 1 egg white
- 2 tablespoons milk
- 1 1/2 tablespoons corn flour
- 2 ounces peas
- 2 Tomatoes
- 2 1/2 cups chicken stock
- 1 -2 tablespoon rice wine or 1 -2 tablespoon dry sherry
- Salt
- White pepper

Directions

1. First of all, take the chicken breast and remove membrane and sinew from it and finely chop it to a paste.

2. Blend with half tbsp. corn flour, milk.

3. Blend in egg whites.

4. After this, skin the tomatoes and chop into small size cubes.

5. Heat the stock to boiling.

6. Add peas.

7. Add tomatoes.

8. When boils once again take away from stove.

9. Drop the chicken mixture into stock by chopsticks.

10. Place the pan back on high temperature setting and heat to boiling again.

11. Take one tbsp. of corn flour and mix with some of water and add this to soup.

12. Add in salt.

13. Add in white pepper.

14. Add in one tbsp. of rice wine.

Boiled Shrimp and Pork Dumplings

Ingredients

- 200 g ground pork
- 100 g shrimp, finely chopped or ground using food processor
- 2 garlic cloves, minced
- 2 green onions, finely chopped
- 1 teaspoon soy sauce
- 1 tablespoon rice wine
- 1/2 tablespoon sesame oil
- 1 teaspoon cornstarch
- 1 teaspoon oyster sauce
- 1/4 teaspoon ground black pepper

- 30 -40 wonton wrappers
- 3 cups chicken stock
- Salt and pepper, to taste (for the stock)
- 1 dash mushroom soy sauce
- Iceberg lettuce (optional) or broccoli (optional)

Directions

1. Mix everything above besides stock and wonton wrappers.
2. Put a tsp of meat mixture in the middle of wrappers.
3. Enclose the filling.
4. Heat the chicken stock to boiling over high temperature setting.
5. Lower the temperature and allow to simmer.
6. Place the dumplings into stock and cook, covered, till dumplings float on surface.
7. Add in the veggies.
8. Add in salt and pepper according to your own choice and taste.

If you enjoy the recipes in this little recipe book, please take the time to share your thoughts and post a review on Amazon. It'd be greatly appreciated!

Thank you and good luck!

Victoria Love
www.AfflatusPublishing.com
www.epicdetox.com
www.secretstoweightlossrevealed.com

Check Out My Other Books

Below you'll find some of my other popular books that are popular on Amazon and Kindle as well. You can visit my author page on Amazon to see other work done by me.

Paleo: The Caveman's Paleo For Beginners: Amazing! The Ultimate Paleo Diet for Beginner's Blueprint for Incredible

Caveman's Revenge Paleo Cookbook: 41 Red Hot Melt The Pounds Fast Weight Loss Recipes Uncovered With Your Top Paleo Diet Questions Answered In Never Before Seen Detail

10 Day Green Smoothie Cleansing: The Ultimate Lose 10 Pounds in 10 Days Green Smoothie Detox Blueprint

10 Day Detox Diet: Innovative Diet Plan Transforms Your Life, Instantly Giving You Explosive Energy and Vitality Guaranteed

Vegetarian Slow Cooker Recipes Revealed: Fast Recipes For Slow Delicious Success

If the links do not work, for whatever reason, you can simply search for these titles on the Amazon website to find them.

Victoria Love

Your *Secret FREE Bonus!*

As a preferred client of Afflatus Publishing we strive to provide more value, all the time. As you are now a special part of our family we want to let you in on a little a little secret...

A special thanks goes out to you. So subscribe to our free e-book giveaway. Each week we will spotlight an amazing new title. Yours absolutely free.

Click Here to Subscribe For Free Now.

http://bit.ly/1aj9JHs